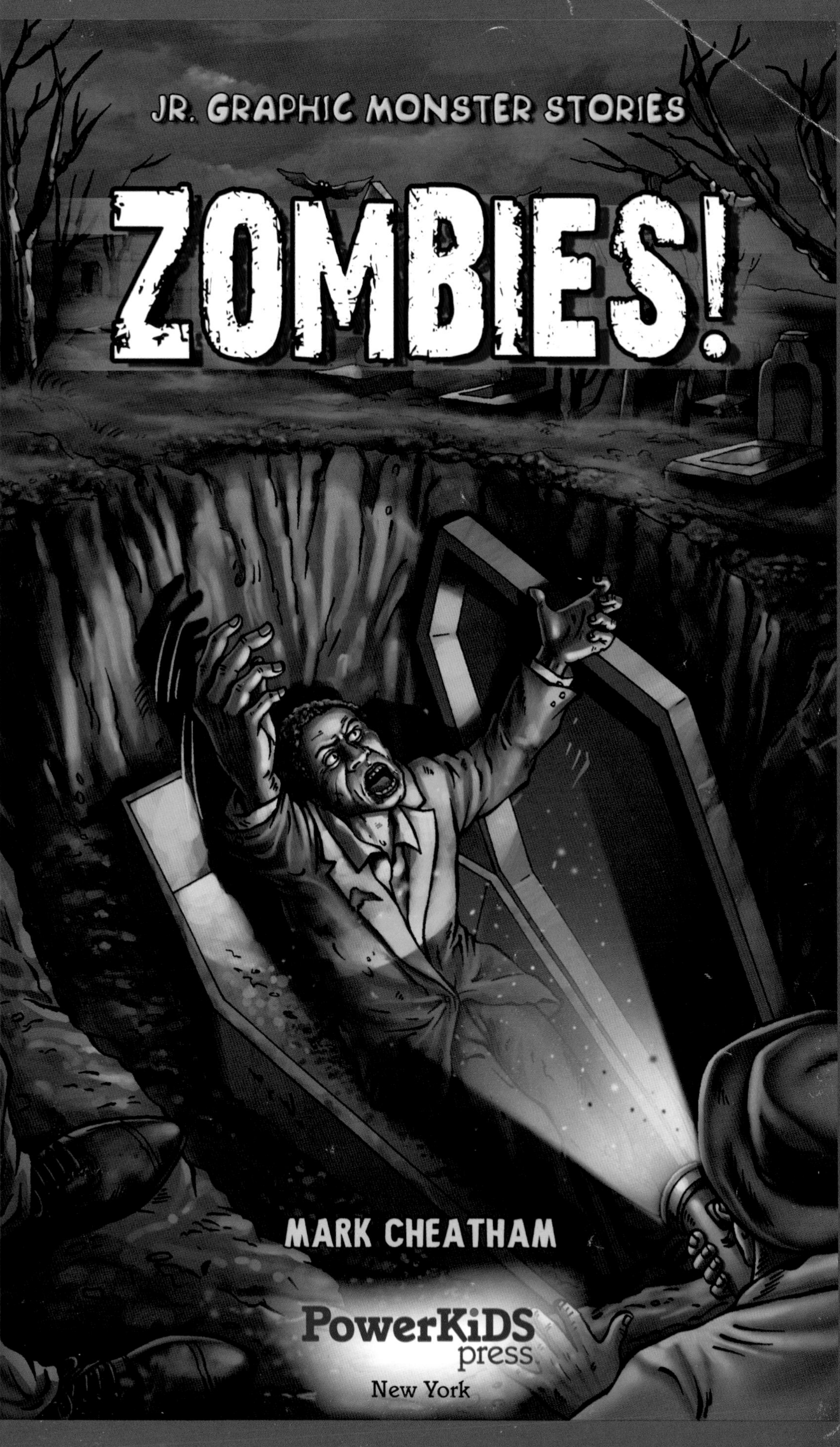
JR. GRAPHIC MONSTER STORIES
ZOMBIES!
MARK CHEATHAM
PowerKiDS press
New York

Published in 2012 by The Rosen Publishing Group, Inc.
29 East 21st Street, New York, NY 10010

First Edition

Editor: Joanne Randolph
Book Design: Planman Technologies
Illustrations: Planman Technologies

Library of Congress Cataloging-in-Publication Data

Cheatham, Mark.
   Zombies! / by Mark Cheatham. — 1st ed.
      p. cm. — (Jr. graphic monster stories)
   Includes index.
   ISBN 978-1-4488-6221-4 (library binding) — ISBN 978-1-4488-6401-0 (pbk.)
   — ISBN 978-1-4488-6402-7 (6-pack)
   1. Zombies—Juvenile literature. I. Title.
   GR830.Z65C53 2012
   398.21—dc23
                              2011022728

Manufactured in the United States of America

CPSIA Compliance Information: Batch #PLW2102PK: For Further Information contact Rosen Publishing, New York, New York at 1-800-237-9932

Contents

Main Characters

Angelina Narcisse Sister of Clairvius Narcisse. Saw her brother declared dead and buried in 1962 yet met him in 1980 in a market.

Clairvius Narcisse (1922–?) Taken under the control of a *bokor*, or zombie master, in Haiti in 1962. Kept captive for two years as a zombie slave, he escaped and was reunited with his family 18 years later.

Zombie Facts

- The zombie experiences of Clairvius Narcisse were studied by Dr. Wade Davis of Harvard University. His book on the subject, *The Serpent and the Rainbow*, was made into a movie in 1988.

- The word "zombie" means "ghost" or "spirit of a dead person" according to Davis.

- In Haiti, a person may be made into a zombie as a punishment for a crime. The people of Haiti do not fear what a zombie will do to them. Instead, they are afraid of being made into a zombie.

- The zombie paste that some bokors feed to their victims is made from a plant called datura or zombie cucumber (called jimson weed or locoweed in the United States). A powerful drug in this plant can cause forgetfulness and a trancelike state. It also can cause people to have a sense of floating outside their bodies.

Zombies!

One weekend afternoon, a man took his daughter and son to a zombie movie.

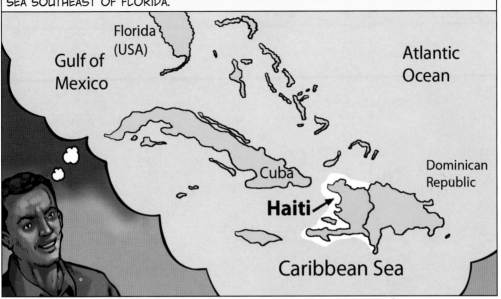

THE STORY BEGINS IN HAITI IN 1980. HAITI IS A NATION ON AN ISLAND IN THE CARIBBEAN SEA SOUTHEAST OF FLORIDA.

ANGELINA NARCISSE WAS SHOPPING AT THE MARKET. A STRANGE-LOOKING MAN CAME UP TO HER. SHE DID NOT KNOW HIM, THOUGH HE LOOKED FAMILIAR.

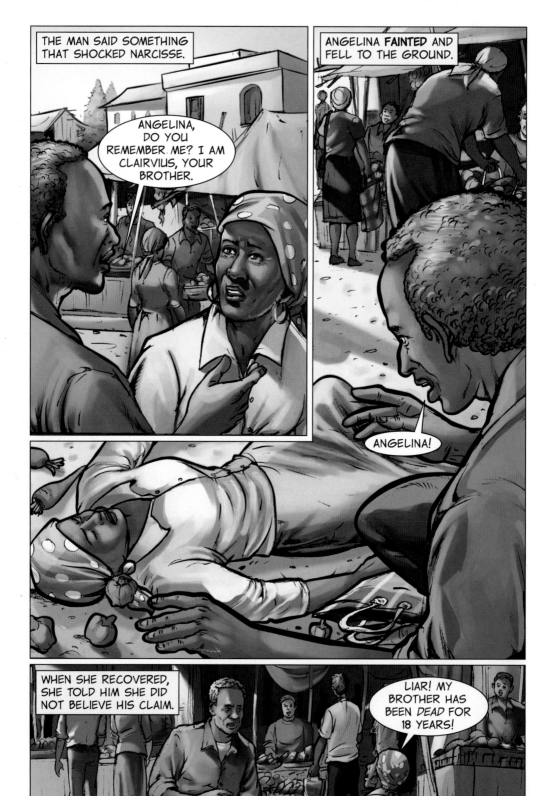

THE MAN SAID SOMETHING THAT SHOCKED NARCISSE.

ANGELINA, DO YOU REMEMBER ME? I AM CLAIRVIUS, YOUR BROTHER.

ANGELINA **FAINTED** AND FELL TO THE GROUND.

ANGELINA!

WHEN SHE RECOVERED, SHE TOLD HIM SHE DID NOT BELIEVE HIS CLAIM.

LIAR! MY BROTHER HAS BEEN *DEAD* FOR 18 YEARS!

THE MAN CONVINCED ANGELINA THAT HE WAS REALLY HER BROTHER BY DESCRIBING THEIR CHILDHOOD TOGETHER.

I BELIEVE YOU *ARE* CLAIRVIUS! BUT HOW CAN YOU BE ALIVE? WE BURIED YOU!

CLAIRVIUS TOLD ANGELINA HIS STORY. IT BEGAN 18 YEARS EARLIER. HE SAID THAT ONE DAY HIS BODY FELT VERY STRANGE. HE WAS SICK TO HIS STOMACH.

DO YOU REMEMBER WHEN YOU TOOK ME TO THE HOSPITAL?

CLAIRVIUS'S SKIN WAS ON FIRE. HE COULD NOT MOVE OR SPEAK. HE COULD HARDLY BREATHE.

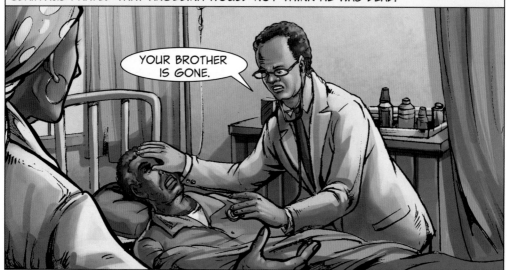

CLAIRVIUS PRAYED THAT ANGELINA WOULD NOT THINK HE WAS DEAD.

YOUR BROTHER IS GONE.

CLAIRVIUS'S HEART HAD SLOWED DOWN SO MUCH THAT THE DOCTOR COULD NOT HEAR IT. CLAIRVIUS COULD NOT MOVE.

OH, NO!

PLEASE, I AM NOT DEAD!

CLAIRVIUS COULD HEAR ANGELINA SOBBING FOR A LONG TIME. THEN A HOSPITAL WORKER WHEELED HIM AWAY TO A COLD, DARK PLACE.

WHEN THEY PUT CLAIRVIUS IN A COFFIN, HE TRIED TO SHOUT THAT HE WAS ALIVE. HE COULD NOT SPEAK.

AT HIS GRAVE, CLAIRVIUS COULD HEAR VOICES FOR A WHILE. HE HEARD DIRT FALLING ON THE COFFIN. HE WAS BEING BURIED ALIVE!

CLAIRVIUS PASSED OUT FOR A TIME. WHEN HE AWOKE, HE FELT AS IF HE WERE FLOATING ABOVE HIS OWN GRAVE. HE WAS BARELY ALIVE.

AM I DEAD?

JUST WHEN HE THOUGHT HE WOULD SURELY DIE, CLAIRVIUS HEARD NOISES ABOVE HIM. HE COULD TELL SOMEONE WAS DIGGING.

AFTER STRANGE MEN TOOK THE LID OFF THE COFFIN, CLAIRVIUS SAT UP. HE COULD JUST BARELY MOVE. HE DID NOT KNOW WHERE HE WAS.

THREE MEN PULLED CLAIRVIUS FROM HIS COFFIN. TO SHOW CLAIRVIUS HE MUST **OBEY** THEM, THEY BEAT HIM WITH STICKS AND THEIR FISTS. THIS ALSO HELPED REVIVE HIM.

PLEASE! STOP!

AFTER THE BEATING, CLAIRVIUS COULD MOVE HIS BODY. THE MEN MADE HIM EAT A **PASTE**. HE REALIZED LATER THAT IT WAS A DRUG THAT TURNED HIM INTO A ZOMBIE. SOON HE BECAME A LIVING DEAD PERSON WITH NO WILL OF HIS OWN.

I AM YOUR BOKOR, YOUR MASTER. YOU WILL DO AS I SAY!

THE MEN BOUND AND GAGGED CLAIRVIUS AND TOOK HIM AWAY.

THEY TOOK CLAIRVIUS TO A SUGAR **PLANTATION**. THERE HE WAS FORCED TO WORK WITH OTHER ZOMBIE **SLAVES**.

GET THIS FIELD CUT OR YOU WILL GET A BEATING!

EVERY DAY THE BOKOR FED THE ZOMBIES A PASTE MADE FROM A PLANT CALLED A ZOMBIE CUCUMBER. THE PASTE WAS A DRUG. IT TOOK AWAY THEIR WILL TO **RESIST**.

THE MASTERS OFTEN BEAT THE ZOMBIES TO GET THEM TO WORK FASTER.

THEN ONE DAY, WHEN ONE OF THE ZOMBIES WAS BEING BEATEN BY THE BOKOR, . . .

. . . THE ZOMBIE STRUCK BACK.

THE BOKOR WAS DEAD. AFTER THE DRUGS WORE OFF, THE ZOMBIES WANDERED AWAY.

CLAIRVIUS WAS LEFT ALONE. HE WANDERED THE COUNTRYSIDE FOR MANY YEARS.

CLAIRVIUS EXPLAINED THAT HE AND HIS BROTHER HAD ARGUED OVER LAND.

THE BOKOR COLLECTED ITEMS TO MAKE A SPECIAL POWDER.

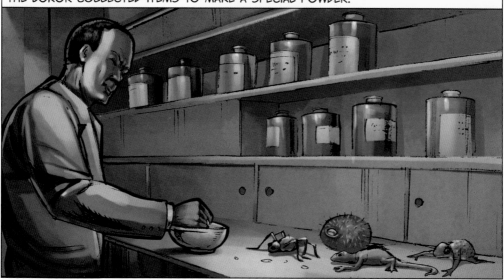

THE BOKOR SAID AN EVIL PRAYER OVER HIS ZOMBIE POWDER. HE THEN GAVE THE POWDER TO CLAIRVIUS'S BROTHER AND TOLD HIM WHAT TO DO.

CLAIRVIUS'S BROTHER SPRINKLED THE POWDER IN CLAIRVIUS'S SHOES AND CLOTHES. IT WOULD WORK ITS WAY INTO CLAIRVIUS'S SKIN AND MAKE HIM SICK.

DOCTORS INVESTIGATED THE CASE OF CLAIRVIUS NARCISSE. THEY TESTED A BOKOR'S DRUGS LIKE THOSE GIVEN TO CLAIRVIUS.

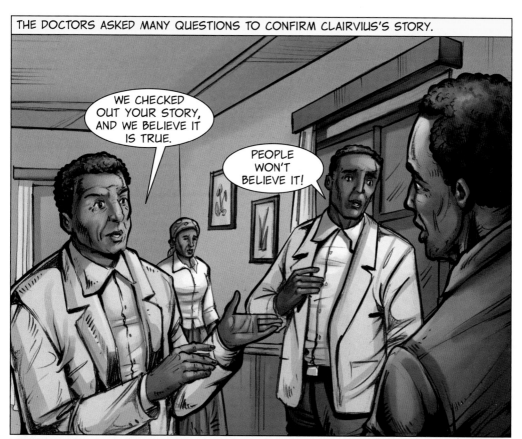

More Zombie Stories

- The word "*zombie*" came into general use after the 1929 publication of the book *The Magic Island* by William B. Seabrook.

  In his book, Seabrook described the "walking dead" he had seen in Haiti. He explained that these zombies had no expressions on their faces. Though not blind, they stared ahead unaware of their surroundings. They seemed to have no will of their own.

- "Papa Doc" Duvalier was dictator of Haiti from 1957 to 1971. His secret police, called Tonton Macoutes, terrorized the people of Haiti. They carried out the orders of Papa Doc without question. The name Tonton Macoutes is from Haitian folklore. It refers to a feared bogeyman who carries off children at night in a gunnysack.

  The Tonton Macoutes wore sunglasses even at night and showed no expressions on their faces. They appeared to be in a trance and completely under the control of their masters. Many Haitians believed that they were zombies. Papa Doc and many important leaders of the Tonton Macoutes were voodoo priests. Many Haitians thought that these leaders were bokors, or zombie masters.

Glossary

bokor (boh-KOR) A priest or witch doctor in the Voodoo religion.

decision (dih-SIH-zhun) The choice a person makes.

fainted (FAYNT-ed) Passed out.

obey (OH-bay) To follow someone's commands.

paste (PAYST) A soft mixture.

plantation (plan-TAY-shun) A very large farm where crops are grown.

resist (rih-ZIST) To work against a force.

slaves (SLAYVZ) People who are "owned" by other people and forced to work for them.

starve (STARV) To suffer or die from hunger.

Timeline for Clairvius Narcisse

- **1962** Narcisse becomes ill and goes to Albert Schweitzer Hospital in Port-au-Prince, Haiti, on April 30 for treatment. He is declared dead on May 2, and buried May 3.

- **1962–1964** Clairvius is taken from his grave and kept as a zombie slave by a witch doctor, or bokor. He is then forced to work in sugarcane fields for two years with other zombies.

- **1964** When the bokor dies, Narcisse escapes the sugarcane plantation with other zombie slaves.

- **1964–1980** Narcisse wanders countryside doing odd jobs.

- **1980** Narcisse reunites with sister Angelina at a marketplace.

- **1982** Doctors find out about the case and investigate. Clairvius's story is found to be true.

Index

Web Sites

Due to the changing nature of Internet links, PowerKids Press has developed an online list of Web sites related to the subject of this book. This site is updated regularly. Please use this link to access the list:

www.powerkidslinks.com/mons/zombies/